Date: 3/29/18

J 796.51 FRI
Frisch, Nate,
Hiking /

PALM BEACH COUNTY
LIBRARY SYSTEM
3650 SUMMIT BLVD.
WEST PALM BEACH, FL 33406

HIKING

HIKING

ODYSSEYS

NATE FRISCH

CREATIVE EDUCATION

Published by Creative Education
P.O. Box 227, Mankato, Minnesota 56002
Creative Education is an imprint of The Creative Company
www.thecreativecompany.us

Design by Blue Design (www.bluedes.com)
Production by Joe Kahnke
Art direction by Rita Marshall
Printed in China

Photographs by Alamy (AF archive, Aurora Photos,
cineclassico, Ed Rhodes, SCPhotos, Stocktrek Images, Inc.,
Greg Vaughn), Creative Commons Wikimedia (Jerome
B. Thompson/Metropolitan Museum of Art/Rogers Fund
1969), iStockphoto (Sava Alexandru, Lysogor), Mary Evans
Picture Library (Kenneth Brookes/The Scout magazine/1934,
INTERFOTO/TV-yesterday), National Geographic Creative
(JOHN BURCHAM), Shutterstock (Africa Studio, Galyna
Andrushko, CebotariN, Daxiao Productions, frantic00,
Izf, Erik Mandre, Alex Sun, wassiliy-architect, Kris Wiktor,
Youproduction), SuperStock (John E Marriott/All Canada
Photos)

Copyright © 2018 Creative Education
International copyright reserved in all countries. No part of
this book may be reproduced in any form without written
permission from the publisher.

Library of Congress Cataloging-in-Publication Data
Names: Frisch, Nate, author.
Title: Hiking / Nate Frisch.
Series: Odysseys in outdoor adventures.
Includes bibliographical references, webography, and index.
Summary: An in-depth survey of the history of hiking, as well
as tips and advice on how to adapt to unexpected situations,
and the skills and supplies necessary for different types of
hiking.
Identifiers: LCCN 2016031803 / ISBN 978-1-60818-688-4
(hardcover) / ISBN 978-1-56660-724-7 (eBook)

Subjects: LCSH: 1. Hiking—Juvenile literature. 2. Hiking—
History—Juvenile literature.
Classification: LCC GV199.52.F75 2017 / DDC 796.51—dc23

CCSS: RI.7.1, 2, 3, 4, 5; RI.8.1, 2, 3, 4, 5; RI.9-10.1, 2, 3, 4; RI.11-12.1,
2, 3, 4; RH.6-8.1, 2, 4, 5; RH.9-10.2, 4, 5

First Edition 9 8 7 6 5 4 3 2 1

CONTENTS

Introduction

Adventure awaits! It's a call from Mother Nature heard by nature lovers and thrill seekers alike. This temptation beckons them, prompting them to pack their gear, pull on their jackets, and head out the door. From mountain peaks to ocean depths and everywhere in between, the earth is a giant playground for those who love to explore and challenge themselves. Not content to follow the beaten

OPPOSITE: With preparation and perseverance, extreme hikers may find their reward atop a mountain summit with a view looking down through the clouds.

path, they push the limits by venturing farther, faster, deeper, and higher. Going to such lengths, they discover satisfaction, excitement, and fun. Theirs is a world of thrilling outdoor adventures.

Hiking may have been the very first adventure for humanity. Ever since, the activity has led people to places both wonderful and terrible. The thrill of hiking has made many people feel more alive, but it has also claimed the lives of others. The unpredictability of events that might occur and sights that may be seen keep adventurous spirits coming back. Tales of such journeys capture the attention of readers, television viewers, and moviegoers. The sport is among the easiest to start, but as distances lengthen, landscapes become unforgiving, weather turns, and wildlife gets defensive, this casual activity can become an extreme challenge.

Humankind's Oldest Sport

However and wherever the first human beings came about, they no doubt had to move around to find food and shelter. Most likely, the first people's primary mode of transportation was their own feet and legs. And they did not have paved sidewalks, roads, or trails. Most definitions of a "hike" refer to an extended walk in natural surroundings. By such measures, the first humans were hikers. The same could be said of any civilization or community whose people walked from place to place in search of food and shelter.

To many, though, "hiking" also suggests an underlying recreational purpose. To these people, hiking is not simply a means of reaching a destination or completing some other task. Instead, the act of walking—while enjoying one's surroundings and possibly socializing—is itself the purpose. According to this more modern perspective, ancient peoples' treks to find food or shelter would not qualify as hiking.

As history progressed, the need to cover long distances was greatly reduced. More and more cultures shifted to a sedentary lifestyle in which people remained at one permanent shelter and raised their own crops and livestock nearby. Most people readily gave up foot travel as animals such as horses and camels were acquired and trained. Technological improvements soon allowed them to build carts, wagons, and other vehicles pulled by animals. By the 1700s, long-distance walking in many advanced countries was thought to be an activity for only armies or poor people. But, again, since these people walked out of necessity rather than as a form of recreation, they were not hikers as we think of them today.

The transition toward modern hiking may have actually begun with quill and ink. As cultures advanced people became less worried about day-to-day survival. They had more time for educational and recreational pursuits. As more people learned to read, they were entertained by published stories that told of strange peoples and lands. Some poets and authors chose to write about natural attractions close to home rather than exotic locales halfway around the globe. Among the first and most successful of these writers was English poet William Wordsworth. Though he did not promote hiking directly, Wordsworth himself toured around Europe in the 1790s. He then poetically described the impressions and feelings he experienced at various shorelines, forests, meadows, brooks, mountains, and valleys. Inspired readers soon sought out these places for their own enjoyment. While a carriage or wagon could get them to their destination in a couple days or less, gaining the fullest experience meant getting out on foot. And so it was that wealthy Europeans stumbling around in fancy hats, dresses, and topcoats ushered in the era of modern hiking.

About a century later, one of America's greatest proponents of hiking came along in the form of John Muir. Unlike Wordsworth, Muir considered himself an amateur naturalist first and a writer second. However, his poetic accounts of the natural wonders in and around California's Yosemite Valley also aroused the interest of the reading public. Those with time and

BELOW *The Belated Party on Mansfield Mountain*, painted by Jerome Thompson in 1858, shows a group of hikers resting and enjoying a picnic after a day trip up Mt. Mansfield in the Green Mountains of Vermont.

money to spend began vacationing in the area. Muir personally led hiking tours for some of these visitors in the late 1800s.

By the early 1900s, wilderness conservation efforts in America were spreading. At the same time, the list of national and state parks was growing. Hiking trails were developed and maintained in most of these parks. They led to some of the most impressive sights while also reducing many of the risks associated with wandering through undeveloped wilderness. Still, hiking remained a hobby mostly for the well-to-do, who often hired guides. On some particularly long trips, the guides would have camps set up along the way where their clients would spend the night.

The booming American economy of the 1920s enabled many families to own automobiles. Average

THE SCOUT
Every Boy's Weekly
2ᵈ

THE SCOUT—EVERY BOY'S WEEKLY   No. 1355   Vol. XXIX   THE ONLY WEEKLY OFFICIAL ORGAN OF THE BOY SCOUTS.   April 14, 1934   Registered for transmission to Canada.   Price 2d.

OPPOSITE Nature-focused organizations such as Boy Scouts and Girl Scouts were formed in the early 1900s to educate children about the outdoors. Typical member activities include camping, backpacking, and completing service projects that improve their communities.

people could quickly travel around the country, and hikers became less dependent on guide services. Both Boy Scouts and Girl Scouts were well established by this time, and appreciation of nature and hiking was being instilled in American youths.

The following decades shifted from an economic crisis in the 1930s, to war in the '40s, to industrial development in the '50s, to civil unrest in the '60s. During this time, progress in hiking and outdoor recreation in general slowed down. But interest flared back up in the 1970s. Recreational camping became common at this time, and more hikers began combining hiking with camping. This blending of activities is often known as backpacking. Backpacking allowed hikers to reach locations that would otherwise be inaccessible on a single-day hike. This popular form of hiking led to changes in the way hiking equipment was made. Backpacks, tents, clothing, and other gear were designed to be more compact and lightweight. These improvements made it easier to carry gear longer distances.

Since the '70s, the sport has continued to evolve. Trails can be found in thousands of national, state, county, and city parks. An entire industry is based on backpacking equipment. Books and websites allow hikers to quickly find and learn about hiking hot spots around the globe. The sport still favors those who have spare money to travel and free time for extended trips, but hiking remains accessible to anyone who is interested.

Room for Luxuries

Backpackers tend to pack light and leave anything considered "nonessential" at home. However, advancements in manufacturing designs and materials have made both essential equipment and nonessential items much lighter and more compact than they used to be. Therefore, today's backpackers can afford to carry a few more luxuries. Some smartphones, e-readers, and other personal devices weigh very little but can put downloaded movies, books, games, and music at a hiker's fingertips. Portable solar-powered battery chargers can keep the devices powered on long trips. Some hikers like having these options once the sun has set or while hunkering down in bad weather. Others think these electronic forms of entertainment conflict with the natural appeal of hiking. Traditional hikers might prefer small paperback books, decks of playing cards, or harmonicas.

Baby Steps and Giant Leaps

Hiking can take place practically anywhere, but elements common to popular hiking destinations include good visibility and varied scenery and experiences. For example, mountainous regions appeal to many hikers. The high points provide impressive overlooks, the lower valleys often contain diverse plant and animal life, and the slopes may feature streams or waterfalls. Hiking near bodies of water is also popular, as shorelines can offer broad vistas of lake or ocean scenery. The water itself attracts many birds and other animals that may otherwise be hard to find. Desert hikes generally offer excellent visibility and can provide stunning surroundings, especially in regions with canyons and other large rock formations.

arks and other places may have trails of less than a quarter-mile (0.4 km). If such paths are paved, they are not usually considered hiking trails. If they are gravel or

dirt, they may represent the simplest end of the hiking spectrum. At the other end are trails that extend for hundreds—or thousands—of miles. The most extreme hikers will take on large sections of these routes. Some will even blaze their own trails through the wilderness. Treks that begin and end in the same day are called day hikes. They may last less than an hour or go from sunup to sundown. Those who go on multi-day hikes are often called backpackers.

Hikers who want to stick to trails can often get trail maps for little or no money. These maps not only show the trail route but also indicate designated backcountry campsites or areas. They often include trail difficulty ratings as well. The rating systems vary by map. Some maps use number scales, while others use words such as "easy" or "strenuous." All factor in distance, difficulty of terrain, and elevation, which can affect oxygen supply. Maps will also list exact distances and perhaps even time estimates for completing a specific hike. Hikers who go off trails, of course, will have no such information. They may choose to use a topographic map or Global Positioning System (GPS) device instead.

Regardless of distance and location, hiking generally puts more strain on the feet than any other part of the body, so selecting good footwear is critical. Where paths are smooth and even, most walking or running shoes are sufficient. For trails that have protruding rocks or tree roots, a hiking shoe, sandal, or boot is a better choice. Hiking shoes may look and feel a lot like running shoes, but their soles are more rigid. Hiking sandals have similar soles, but their open upper design makes them more breathable and quick-drying. Hiking boots have the sturdiest soles. Plus, the upper part of the boot provides more ankle support and protection from thorns or poking twigs. They are a good all-around choice for on- and off-trail hiking in various conditions.

Trekking poles can work in tandem with good footwear to improve a hiking experience. Resembling ski poles, they reduce the amount of weight your lower body has to support. This lessens strain on the joints and muscles. They also improve balance and grip on uneven or slippery surfaces.

Proper gear is an important part of the hiking experience. For those traversing rocky or slippery areas, trekking poles and waterproof hiking boots are essential for balance and stability—not to mention keeping feet dry.

Other equipment for day hikers might include extra clothing, water bottles, snacks, toilet paper, and first-aid supplies. Backpackers add to this list. They might pack hygiene items, cookware, shelters, sleeping bags and pads, and repair or emergency items such as rope, duct tape, and knives. Hauling a lot of stuff and walking long distances don't naturally go well together, so finding ways to reduce bulk is a priority for serious hikers.

It's recommended to carry no more than 20 percent of your body weight. To accomplish this, try to choose compact, lightweight versions of what you need. Also think about how each object could serve multiple purposes. For example, instead of a bulky coat, several lighter layers of clothing can be combined to suit any weather

Trial Run

An extended backpacking trip takes careful preparation and equipment selection. Putting plans and checklists on paper is a good start, but some problems may not be evident until plans are put into practice. New hiking boots may cause blisters. Layers of clothing that fit well individually may not be comfortable when all worn together. The back of a wide-brimmed hat may keep hitting a tall backpack. Also, new backpackers may not realize how heavy a pack can feel after miles of walking on rugged terrain. Hikers should take a few shorter hikes—ideally in diverse weather conditions—with their entire assortment of equipment (including a full pack) before relying on it for a multi-day hike.

condition. A headlamp is smaller and more versatile than a lantern, and a small cooking pot can also be used as a bowl or cup. Many backpackers take dehydrated and freeze-dried foods, which are easy to carry and store.

Backpackers are choosy when it comes to shelters and sleep systems. Backpacking shelters vary, but almost all of them pack up small. Freestanding tents have a complete framework of poles that keep the tent erect. They are usually enclosed with built-in floors. Non-freestanding tents may use just a pole or two and rely on stakes and tie-out lines to keep the structure upright. Many are designed to pitch with trekking poles in place of extra tent poles. They may or may not have floors. If shelters don't have floors, people may use a waterproof ground cloth or a sort of full-body shell called a bivouac sack, or "bivy." Some backpackers use only a bivy for shelter.

Hammock-style bivies are an option as well, but they require the use of sturdy, well-positioned trees.

A sleep system usually consists of a sleeping bag plus a mat or pad of some sort. The sleeping bags that offer the most warmth for their weight are mummy bags. Mummy bags conform closely to a person's body. Those stuffed with down feathers are a little lighter than comparable bags with manmade insulation. Foam mats are lightweight and provide insulation between a person and the ground. However, good inflatable pads can be just as light, pack smaller, insulate better, and offer more cushion. The tradeoff is higher cost and the possibility of springing a leak.

Any hiker who has a lot to carry will want a pack. Daypacks look like school backpacks, but may be trimmer and more adjustable for a secure fit. Hydration packs feature an interior water pouch with a long, flexible straw. The wearer can sip from the straw without removing the pack. Some day hikers prefer belt-like waist or lumbar packs. These packs save their shoulders and allow better airflow to the back.

Backpackers usually need bigger packs to accommodate everything they need. Storage capacity is typically measured in liters, ranging from about 20 liters (5.3 gal) for a day trip to more than 50 (13.2 gal) for a multi-day hike. Modern packs are made of light, waterproof materials and feature strap padding and adjustability for a good fit. Perhaps most beneficial is that they strap around the waist in addition to the shoulders. This makes the pack seem lighter and keeps the spring in one's step longer.

BELOW While many recreational backpackers strive for packs as light as 10 pounds (4.5 kg), military **infantry** often train and travel with packs weighing upwards of 70 pounds (31.8 kg).

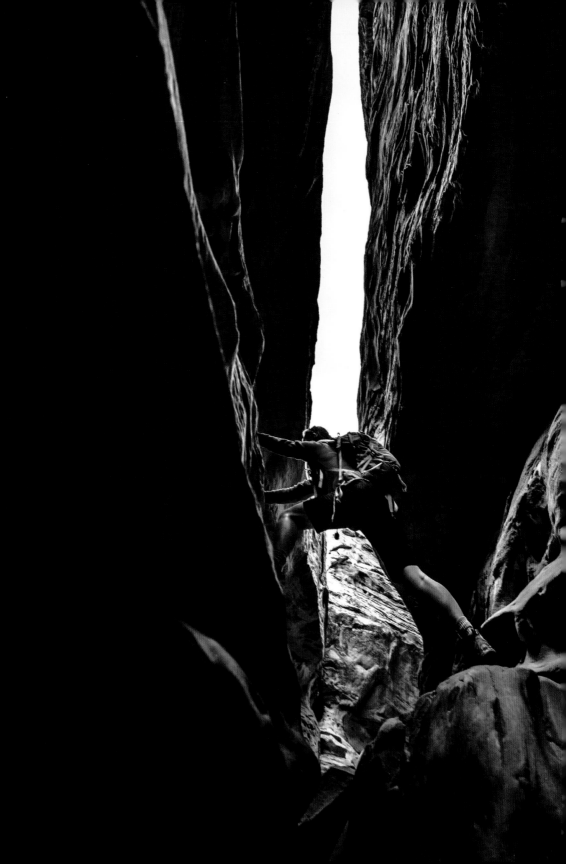

Just a Walk ... Isn't It?

To an observer, hiking may not seem to be especially risky. However, on backpacking trips, hikers may become far removed from the safety net of civilization. One weary misstep on unstable terrain can sprain an ankle or knee or break a bone. Such an injury can leave hikers in the middle of nowhere with limited water and food, and their only means of transportation—their legs—damaged.

OPPOSITE: More advanced hikes may consist of climbing rocks, scaling cliffs, or squeezing through narrow passageways. Hikers should travel in groups to prevent getting lost and to help if someone suffers from illness or injury.

erhaps the best safety measure any hiker can take is to travel with someone. Having one companion is good, having more is generally even better. If one person is injured or ill, others can administer first aid or get help. If one hiker's equipment is damaged or inadequate, another may be able to share. In extreme cold, multiple people huddled together retain heat better than an individual. Groups are also at lesser risk from predator attacks, and they become lost less often. Having others around also improves morale. In the event a hike turns into a survival situation, maintaining hope can be the difference between life and death.

As for more specific safety measures, a combination of supportive hiking boots, trekking poles, and a light pack will reduce risk of injury, but sensible choices during the

hike are just as important. Staying on trails often ensures safer footing than hiking off-trail. Wading through a shallow stream is frequently safer than hopping from one slippery rock to another or trying to use a narrow, wet log as a bridge. Selecting a more gradual, winding route up or down a mountain may be slow but can be wiser than rushing along the most direct path. Tired hikers are more prone to accidents, so breaking for rest, water, and food is recommended over long distances. Backpackers should also make camp when fading sunlight hinders their ability to see their footing.

TAKEAWAY

Hikers should be prepared for both warmer and colder conditions than expected for any given trip.

Making good choices of when and where to hike is the best way to deal with extreme heat or cold. Extensive summertime backpacking in a desert invites trouble, as do multi-day hikes in mountains during winter. But even sensible locations at sensible times of year can yield nasty weather. Hikers should be prepared for both warmer and colder conditions than expected for any given trip. General guidelines for being adaptable include selecting multiple clothing layers that can be added or removed as necessary. Clothing should also have zippers, buttons, drawstrings, or other fasteners that can be adjusted to release or retain body heat. Having the option to cover most of your skin as protection from the sun, cold, or biting bugs is also wise for extended hikes.

When temperatures rise, many people's natural

OPPOSITE It is important to purify drinking water from natural sources, such as rivers and lakes. Even if it looks, smells, or tastes clean, this water can contain bacteria and pollutants that cause nausea, diarrhea, fever, and chills.

reaction is to shed clothing and expose more skin to the air. But direct sunlight can actually make a hiker feel hotter. Lightweight pants with zip-off legs and a buttoned, long-sleeved shirt over a T-shirt are good options for warm to hot conditions. Hats with full brims can provide shade, and—along with sunglasses—greatly benefit one's eyes as well.

Warm-weather hikers also need a lot of water—a quart (0.9 l) or more per hour in hot temperatures—to stay hydrated. In places where natural fresh water is available, hikers should boil or filter the water before drinking. This will rid it of harmful bacteria and parasites. In places where water is not available or contains dirt that can't be filtered out, hikers must carry more water, heavy though it may be. In dry regions, the flesh of most cacti is good to eat and contains moisture. This can help

What's in a Material?

Cotton is among the most common and comfortable materials used in people's everyday clothing. And for pleasant, dry weather, it's not a bad choice for hiking, either. However, when moisture—from rain, sweat, condensation, or stream crossings—enters the equation, cotton loses its insulating properties and is slow to dry. This can leave a hiker either hot and sticky or cold and clammy. Wool, on the other hand, can insulate even when wet. But it, too, dries slowly. Many synthetic fabrics wick, or pull away, moisture from the skin and allow that moisture to evaporate quickly. Synthetic fleece garments are often thick and insulate well, but wind can easily blow through them. This problem can be solved with wind-blocking materials such as nylon.

in a pinch, but it won't offer long-term hydration. Resting in the shade in the hottest parts of the day and hiking at cooler times is also beneficial for regulating water use.

At the other extreme, cold-weather hikers need more layers for warmth. Four layers is common for the upper body, and two is common for the lower body. The base, or innermost, layer is often a close-fitting thermal shirt and pants. Two additional layers of fleece or other synthetic material are commonly worn on the upper body. A water- and windproof jacket and pants make up the outermost layer. Layering gloves and weatherproof mittens is also recommended, and a stocking hat or balaclava can combine with the hood of the outer jacket to handle various conditions. Wraparound sunglasses or ski goggles not only reduce glare from snow but can block chilling wind as well.

If boots aren't insulated, socks made of good insulating material such as wool are especially important. But extra-thick socks can prove counterproductive. When squeezed into a boot, the fibers compress and lose their insulating properties. This can also squish blood vessels in the foot and reduce circulation that is essential for spreading warmth throughout the body. Layers on the rest of the body shouldn't be too snug for the same reason.

Clothing can also repel stings and bites from bugs and snakes. Hikers in venomous snake territory sometimes wear gaiters, which cover a person's lower legs and—along with good boots—ward off fangs. Ticks may seem less threatening, but if they are able to bite a hiker's skin, some types can transmit long-lasting illnesses. Hiking in light-colored clothing can make ticks easier to spot. Tucking shirts into waistbands and pant legs into socks limits access to the skin. Insect repellent also makes ticks less interested in grabbing on.

oise is the best deterrent for threats such as bears. Most large animals will avoid people if they have

OPPOSITE If you are hiking outside of city limits, you could encounter wild animals. Most will generally avoid people, but you should have a plan in place so that you know what to do if one crosses your path.

enough warning. Many hikers in bear country wear bells on their packs, clothing, or walking sticks for this reason. If big animals are encountered and become aggressive, cans of bear spray, which are like oversized pepper spray, may be the most portable and effective line of defense.

Animal encounters, washouts, floods, or other unexpected events can force hikers off trails, so having maps and compasses and knowing how to use them is critical. GPS devices can serve the same purpose, but they are often expensive and can break or lose power.

Enjoying Others' Hardships

As much as a hiker hopes he never faces life-or-death conditions in the wilderness, such situations can make for irresistible entertainment. One might be hard pressed to find a popular book, TV show, or movie that recounts a pleasant, predictable, recreational hike. But on-foot journeys full of danger, setbacks, and unexpected twists have been a part of storytelling since before written history.

OPPOSITE: Many people enjoy stories of adventure, with characters overcoming challenging or dangerous obstacles. These stories are entertaining, but they can also be educational, as readers can learn from the characters' mistakes.

Whether to explain the world around them, to teach lessons, or simply to entertain, oral tales of eventful treks have been passed down from generation to generation in many cultures. Early examples of written stories include Greek myths such as Homer's *Odyssey* or the tales of Jason and the Argonauts. The mythical heroes frequently travel by ship, but at times they cover long distances on foot, facing deadly challenges along the way.

Long walks and prolonged wandering tend to be a recurring theme in religious scripts as well. In the Old Testament books that inform the religious traditions of Christianity, Judaism, and Islam, the first direct mention of God being on Earth comes in the book of Genesis: Adam and Eve hear God walking in the Garden of Eden after they eat the forbidden fruit. Other major events of the Old Testament involve Abraham and, later, Moses hiking up mountains and speaking with God. Eventually, Moses and his followers are forced to wander in the desert for 40 years as punishment for ill deeds. This story is reflected in the Christian gospels when Jesus wanders in the desert for 40 days by himself, without food, praying and withstanding temptations of the devil.

These accounts suggest that a long journey can be both a penance and a means of spiritual enlightenment. Even today, Muslims make pilgrimages on foot to Mecca in Saudi Arabia. Hindus also undertake pilgrimages to

BELOW In the Old Testament of the Bible, the Israelites followed Moses as they wandered in the desert for 40 years before arriving in the land promised them by God.

designated holy places. Various peoples throughout the world, such as many American Indian tribes, traditionally required young men to strike out on their own into the wilderness until they received a vision or some other type of spiritual awakening.

nglish author Charles Dickens renewed the idea of wandering as a form of penance in his 1843 book, *A Christmas Carol*. In this story, the ghost of Jacob Marley is forced to wander the earth for eternity as punishment for his misdeeds in life. He warns the foul-tempered

Ebenezer Scrooge to change his ways in order to avoid the same fate.

Jules Verne's 1864 science fiction novel *Journey to the Center of the Earth* was more in line with the adventurous sentiments of Greek mythology. The French author portrayed foot travel as having limitless possibilities. His story follows a professor and his nephew as they venture deep underground and encounter prehistoric animals and other strange phenomena. Verne's work likely inspired other fantasy adventures such as J. R. R. Tolkien's *The Lord of the Rings* series and C. S. Lewis's *The Chronicles of Narnia*. Each book follows the protagonists' travels and exploits—mostly afoot—across vast, dangerous worlds. Both series were later turned into movies. In 1933, *King Kong* was among the first films to capitalize on the suspense and excitement of having vulnerable characters

BELOW In 1933's *King Kong*, a film director takes his cast and crew to a secluded island to make a movie. The group treks through the jungle, swinging from vines and crossing dangerous terrain before encountering dinosaurs and a giant gorilla.

trek through unpredictable, inhospitable lands.

While such fantasy adventures have long remained popular, factual accounts related to hiking have also entertained readers for many years. John Muir's *My First Summer in the Sierra* (1911) describes his early impressions and experiences in California's Yosemite Valley. Across the globe, Jim Corbett, a conservationist who also hunted man-eating tigers and leopards in India, wrote several books from the early to mid-1900s. Though his books are not specifically about hiking, Corbett's efforts to track animals resulted in his walking thousands of miles over the forested Himalayan foothills. His detailed accounts of the rugged land and his experiences with and knowledge of its wildlife often overshadowed the hunting aspects of his tales. More recently, adventurer and author Mark Jenkins has written books about his journeys around the world. In addition to foot travel, his adventures include bicycling, boating, and horseback riding.

Aless successful true-life adventure tale involved Christopher Mc-Candless. A novice backpacker who ventured into the Alaskan wilderness in 1992, Mc-Candless eventually died from eating a poisonous plant. His story was the basis for the 2007 movie *Into the Wild*. Other films that involve hiking in one way or another include the fictional *Stand by Me*. Released in 1986, the movie follows four 12-year-old boys who set out on foot to find a missing person (or the body of a missing person) they heard about on the news. The 2011 film *The Way* is among the very few films that are specifically about hiking. *The Way* depicts a father attempting a long hike in France after his son died on the very same trail. These three films could all be classified as adventure movies, but they also relate to the idea of wandering as a search for enlightenment.

Television shows devoted specifically to hiking are also a rarity, but survival shows such as *Man vs. Wild* and *Dual Survival* became popular in the early 2000s. Such programs often show their stars or hosts hiking through hazardous terrain, such as murky swamps, scorching deserts, scree-covered hillsides, slick glaciers, or dense forests. Along the way, they demonstrate how to keep cool, warm, or dry as needed, how to get one's bearings if lost, and how to find water, food, and shelter in emergencies.

BELOW Actor Emile Hirsch portrayed Christopher McCandless in the 2007 film *Into the Wild*. McCandless spent nearly four months living alone in the Alaskan wilderness before dying of food poisoning and starvation. He left behind a camera and a journal documenting his time in the wild.

Major Trails Near Home

Most Americans don't have to travel far to find some type of hiking trail. Driving a day or less can lead most hikers to one of five major trail systems. In the East is the Eastern Continental Trail, which runs from Florida to Newfoundland, Canada. It also contains the mountainous Appalachian Trail. In the West, the Pacific Crest Trail runs 2,650 miles (4,265 km) through the U.S. from the Mexican to the Canadian border. It meanders through both the Sierra Nevada and Cascade mountain ranges. The Continental Divide Trail also follows mountains—the Rockies in this case—from Mexico to Canada. Lengthy east-to-west trails include the North Country Trail, which extends from New York through the upper Midwest into North Dakota. Longest of them all is the 6,800-mile (10,944 km) American Discovery Trail. This system of trails spans the entire nation, from Delaware to California.

Starting Down the Path

The predominant draw of hiking is simply to get out in nature and experience the sights, sounds, and fresh air that goes with it. Many birdwatchers follow hiking paths that may lead to elusive species. Artists and photographers may hike in search of beautiful scenes to capture. Other hikers hit the trails for the sake of exercise.

Whatever the reason for it, hiking is

OPPOSITE: Hiking can be a fun and easy way to experience nature in a new way, whether you are exploring a national park or walking along a river close to home. You can start out on a short, level trail, or head to the hills for a steeper climb.

among the easiest activities to get into. Unless you live in the middle of a big city, most people don't have to go far to reach a natural park or preserve with some trails running through it. Both males and females ranging from young children to elderly enjoy casual forms of the sport. Supportive footwear and trekking poles enable even people with knee, hip, or foot pain to participate to some extent.

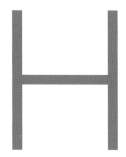ikers who want to share their interest with others, learn from fellow hikers, and give back to the sport

BELOW Regular hiking provides health benefits. Physical activity reduces anxiety, lowers the risk of heart disease, and strengthens bones against osteoporosis. Hiking also provides a different setting to spend time with friends or family members.

Extreme Backpacking Races

Backpacking can be challenging enough as it is. When it's done as a race, the difficulty level increases. To finish near the front, competitors have to run, and some races cover more than 100 miles (161 km). The conditions aren't necessarily pleasant, either. Racers in Canada's Yukon Arctic Ultra cover up to 300 miles (483 km) of wilderness in February temperatures of around 0 °F (-18 °C). In Brazil's 158-mile (254 km) Jungle Marathon, competitors face stifling heat and cross rivers with piranhas, anacondas, and **caimans**. The route of Italy's Tor des Géants (Tour of Giants) goes from mountain to mountain. Participants climb and descend more than 1.2 vertical miles (2 km) at least 25 times. Simply finishing these "ultra runs" is an achievement. Every year, competitors throughout the world are hospitalized.

they love may join the American Hiking Society (AHS). AHS members often form volunteer groups that develop and maintain hiking trails across the country. Costs for tools and other materials are covered by membership fees. Joining such a group can be a great way for a novice hiker to learn more about backpacking or rigorous day hikes.

Serious hiking that covers many miles is not for everyone. It can require great stamina, especially when loads are heavy and terrain is rough. Extended hikes may also require the mental toughness to endure bad

OPPOSITE In mountainous regions, hungry hikers can use nature to their advantage, building fires beneath rocks to create a surface on which to cook or warm food in pots.

weather and general aches and weariness. Backpackers in particular simply need to be willing to do without comforts of home. The best sleep systems are still less comfortable than an average bed. Freeze-dried meals can get old quickly, and restrooms amount to taking a roll of toilet tissue behind a bush. Bath and laundry services exist only where rivers, streams, or lakes are present.

Another requirement for effective backpacking is either to spend a decent amount of money on equipment or to have the creativity and patience to make or acquire it on the cheap. Buying a full checklist of new gear that is both light and of high quality is expensive. The total cost of a top-end tent, sleeping bag, pad, backpack, cookware, mini-stove, apparel, trekking poles, water filter, and boots would be enough to furnish a modern living room with nice furniture and an entertainment system!

Fortunately, materials are available to make some of your own equipment, and plans for such projects can easily be found online. Tyvek is a waterproof, breathable construction material available at many building supply stores and online. Thrifty backpackers have found that it works well for homemade shelters, bivies, rain apparel, and even backpacks. All that is generally needed is some ingenuity and maybe some duct tape, parachute cord, and wooden dowels or rods.

For items that are hard to make, finding alternatives to the pricey equipment is another option. For example, water-treatment tablets come in little jars that are much cheaper (and more compact) than portable filtration systems. Squat food cans, such as those that beef stew often comes in, are about the same size and weight as personal titanium cook pots. Once any sharp edges are smoothed out, they can serve the same role. A cat food tin with some holes punched in the side and alcohol as fuel can become a cheap, ultralight burner.

When nothing but the real item will do, used equipment that is in almost-new condition can be bought at a much lower price. Also, some manufacturers put out slightly revised versions of tents, sleeping bags, and apparel every year (even if the only difference is in color or logo placement). Because of this, backpackers can often get big discounts on leftover items from the previous year.

Finally, just as reducing the number of things in the bag cuts down on bulk and weight, it also reduces costs. For example, rather than buying a camping pillow, many backpackers will simply cram the fleece jacket they already have into the stuff sack their sleeping bag or pad just came out of to make a pillow.

The happiest hikers take in every little moment of the trek rather than focus on just getting to the end of a trail.

erhaps even more than one's physical abilities and one's equipment, it is the difference in perspective and composure that separates those who enjoy the extreme versions of hiking from those who do not. A common saying states that "life is a journey, not a destination." This can easily be applied to hiking. The happiest hikers take in every little moment of the trek rather than focus on just getting to the end of a trail. They keep their senses

alert to their surroundings and are willing to stop and appreciate the sights, sounds, smells, and feel of the air and objects around them—even if it means being delayed or changing course from time to time. If your only goal on a hike is simply to move from one place to another, the hours in between can feel like a long, tiresome chore.

A sudden downpour would send many hikers home. But an extreme hiker is more likely to hunker down and enjoy the sounds and smell of the rain and the mysterious gray veil it casts over a landscape. After a poor night's sleep on the ground, some backpackers may grumble about aches and pains, while others will be all the more eager to hit the trails and work loose any soreness. And so, in the end, being an extreme hiker is not about performing incredible feats but simply about taking everything in stride.

Glossary

backcountry   an area that is away from developed or populated areas

balaclava   cold-weather headgear that covers the head and neck and leaves only part of the face exposed

caimans   predatory tropical reptiles closely related to crocodiles and alligators

freeze-dried   referring to food or other substances that are frozen and then have water molecules removed by altering the pressure around the substance

infantry   soldiers trained to travel and fight on foot

morale   the mental or emotional well-being of an individual or group; often referring to a combination of confidence, enthusiasm, and determination

penance   a generally difficult or unpleasant task performed to express regret or make up for previous wrongdoings

pilgrimages   journeys undertaken for spiritual or religious reasons; often ending at sacred places or shrines

scree   collective layers of broken rock that form on the slopes and base of crumbling hills or cliffs

sedentary   settled in one place

| synthetic | describing a material that is not found in nature but created through chemical processes |
| topographic map | a map which shows the layout and general shape of a land area based on variations in elevation |

Selected Bibliography

Berger, Karen. *America's Great Hiking Trails*. New York: Rizzoli, 2014.

Curtis, Rick. *The Backpacker's Field Manual: A Comprehensive Guide to Mastering Backcountry Skills*. New York: Three Rivers Press, 2005.

Gerke, Randy. *Outdoor Survival Guide*. Champaign, Ill.: Human Kinetics, 2010.

McManners, Hugh. *The Backpacker's Handbook*. New York: Dorling Kindersley, 1995.

National Geographic Guide to the National Parks of the United States. 6th ed. Washington, D.C.: National Geographic Society, 2009.

Sweeney, Michael S. *National Geographic Complete Survival Manual*. Washington, D.C.: National Geographic Society, 2008.

Tawrell, Paul. *Wilderness Camping & Hiking*. Lebanon, N.H.: Exxa LLC, 2007.

Townsend, Chris. *The Backpacker's Handbook*. 4th ed. Chicago: McGraw-Hill, 2012.

Websites

Backpacking Lightweight
www.backpacking.net

This site includes information about many backpacking topics, including checklists, guides on selecting equipment, and even directions on how to make your own.

Trails.com
www.trails.com/

Trails.com is a resource for finding some of the most popular trails in the U.S. and Canada. Maps and information including length, difficulty, and reviews are provided for each trail listed.

Note: Every effort has been made to ensure that any websites listed above were active at the time of publication. However, because of the nature of the Internet, it is impossible to guarantee that these sites will remain active indefinitely or that their contents will not be altered.

Index